Published 2019

Copyright – Marcelle Mae © (& Sarah Camille)

All rights reserved. No production, copy or transmission of the publication may be made without written permission.
No paragraph of this publication may be reproduced, copied or transmitted save with written approval of the Australian Copyright Act 1956 (as amended) and as permitted by US copyright law.

www.marcellemae.com

ISBN: 9780648530015

111

preface	5
prompt	7
perhaps	8

- - - - - - - - - - - - - - - -

revelation	10
realisation	30
reclamation	64
remuneration	86
realignment	92

- - - - - - - - - - - - - - - -

permission slip	109
release	111

determiner: enough; pronoun: enough
as much or as many as required.
"too much work and not enough people to do it"
sufficient, adequate, ample, abundant, as much ...
as necessary, the necessary;
insufficient - used to indicate that one is unwilling to
tolerate any more of something undesirable
"we've got enough problems without them"
sufficient, adequate, ample, abundant, as much ...
as necessary, the necessary;
informal plenty of
"do we have enough commitment?"
insufficient
adverb: enough - to the required degree or extent
(used after an adjective, adverb, or verb).
"before he was old enough to value loyalty"
to a moderate degree; fairly
"he could get there easily enough"
sufficiently, adequately, amply, satisfactorily,
passably, tolerably, reasonably, fairly
" he gave her just enough "
"in large enough numbers, men can create change"
Insufficiently - used for emphasis.
" curiously enough, there is no mention of him "

Dedication

*For all those who trusted and were deceived,
by the trapdoor falls of unfulfilling lies,
calling on the power of alchemy,
taking wings from pain, creating butterflies;*

*here's to the darkness of the processing tunnel,
where we find all the diamonds in the rough;
here's to your light and your power,
credit to you, you are brave enough*

Preface:

The cabin crew have just finished their safety warning. All the passengers sit in limbo. Not moving. Just waiting. Sitting on the tarmac. Just standing. Just being. Waiting. Waiting for instructions. Waiting to be moved. Under the cover of chatter, I summon up the courage to spill the beans. Well, isn't this ironic, sitting next to my girlfriend in the emergency row, telling her about my crisis.

"So...", I say. She turns to look at me. " I'll tell you a story. BUT I do not need you to do anything about it. I do not need your opinion on it. I just need to tell you. You just need to know."

She has known me long enough to know that what I am about to say could literally be anything. From winning tattslotto, to travelling to Antarctica, becoming an astronaut, to being diagnosed with cancer. I thrive on the changing pace of life, moving often and changing the furniture in my house even more often. I am at heart a gypsy, and I am a Gemini. I spin many plates, and juggle more tasks than I know I can handle. Some like security, I like venturing into the unknown, and all be it unprepared.

I continue. "Once upon a time, there was a girl who fell in love with a boy. They were together for nine years before he proposed to her. They married and had three children. They moved interstate, travelled to America for work, and took a family world trip on the return home; including Paris, the city of love. They have been together for 16 years…

She has just found out he cheated on her three times before they were married, and had never told her. She married a lie. She birthed three children with it. She is unsure of what she is doing, where she is going, and how she is going to get there. She has never been more present in her life and never been more lost." I smile awkwardly before continuing. "Yes, I know I am in the shit and probably need your help and other people's advice more than I can allow, but this is my thing to handle".

This is the defiance of a woman who spent her life being the listener, the carer, the giver. Validated by not putting her problems on others, being able to handle things personally, being quiet, fitting in and making life easier for others. Being unseen and unheard.

I am not alone. Many of us receive these crushing gifts, so that we can be birthed back into ourselves; to restart living out our own values, ensuring our own happiness, on our terms.

A generation that yearns to be seen will learn to see themselves. Through the pain of being pulled apart and reassembled, we find our power. Through the unravelling we reclaim our voices and proclaim our own worth, and that enough is enough.

In my efforts to be seen and not heard, I had begun listening to, and filling my sense of self with fractions of others. I had replaced my voice with theirs. In doing so I had formed a fractured sense of self. I had begun to evaluate myself on their terms. I had permitted them to rule me, evaluate me, and use and discard me.

We were returning from a weekend away at Lake St Clair in Tasmania. A divine pump house come unique hotel. The hotel is 150 metres into the lake, with water lapping at the sides of the building, views of snow-capped mountains, surrounded with bush land and ever green lush foliage. Inside, cozy wood fires invite you to lounge on generous, soft couches, complete with blankets and pillows. Before settling in for an afternoon siesta or to take in a book, guests pour themselves a Tasmanian red, a warming whisky or drink of choice, Cointreau on ice, from the open bar.

A literal 'get away', in both the physical and mental senses. Allowing myself 'time away' and 'self-love' is a new notion for me. One that becomes a permanent part of my life. To be heard. To be loved. To be seen. By myself. As I am.

Here's to reclaiming our voices.

Prompt:

what are you healing from? what are you undressing?
maybe they are your words? your actions?
maybe they were theirs? the ones that cut you?
maybe you think your choices allowed them to do what they have done? maybe you don't like confrontation?
maybe this is not the end, but the beginning?
maybe their actions are a gift? in the long term?
maybe it just is. or was? an event out of your control?
maybe you won't call it anxiety? or depression? too cliché?
maybe you'll think it is just another hard day?
maybe you hear the words planted inside your head?
planted by somebody else's voice?
the friend. the family. the parents. society's imposed self-introspection, with a filter of "too this, too that"
... money, beauty, muscles, expression, personality,
skin colour, clothes, noise, material, emotions ...
the words in your head.. the sit, stay still, don't talk, follow instructions. the too loud, too demanding, too emotional, too sensitive, too hard, too soft, too needy. too religious. too strong. too different. the too much ... or the too little... the can't you do more, be more, say more, give more. the not enough effort, the not skinny enough, not helpful enough, not convenient enough, not easy enough, just not enough. The be what I want you to be, be less of you and be more like me. the be as I say, not as I do...
and once i've broken you, be who you are ... or who you were. if you can? remember?

Perhaps?

because I was a good girl,
because I was straight laced,
because I was trusting and naïve,
because I was tall, and not tall enough,
because I was pretty, and not pretty enough,
because I didn't speak up, because I was too loud,
because I flicked my hair, because I was inhibited,
because I was shy, because I was vain,
because I was fast, because I was slow,
because I was indoctrinated, because they said so…
(too loud, too messy, too demanding)
because I couldn't (do the splits)
because I could (be loyal)
because I had standards
because I was emotional
because I was "tete en l'air"…
because I had my head in the clouds
because I was grounded
because I was a woman
because I was a mother
because all that I was…
I was measured against external expectations.

revelation

i invited a devil to rise at my door
asked him to bring three deceits to explore
he hid my groom in a candour of white
when petrol fumes should have burnt up the night
and so in my love's sudden switching veil
i was quartered and sectioned, and cut to impale
a quarter for me, so the others could be -
my daughters divine, all mine ...
so they cancelled out well
one for each time he'd fell -
i had a scar for each birth needing healing
i basted with, each tormented feeling ...
and i'd thought i'd be free, with my three equals three
but it's hard to unsee ...
trusts shattered expression, loves hurtful regression
the raw pains infliction, his willing addiction
to cast down my worth, his angel on earth
that he banished to hell, like some object to sell ...

in spite that I'd loved him so well

canvas

he was as real and as hollow as a dream.

the sweetest thing I have never seen.

my everything.

that's never been.

a canvas painted

and yet clean

*i imagined the world would have exploded
when you told me of your deception*

*i felt my heart shatter and my trust fracture ...
and yet a pin dropping would have pierced the silence in
that moment*

*the astonishment and disbelief that my strongest
supporter was, in fact, my harshest critic*

*that the man who had vowed to love me till death
had in fact, already killed me*

premonition

she woke in fear
that the love she had given was in vain
that all the trust she had offered
had rendered her insane

she stopped waiting on other people
sitting
wanting
wishing

and found again inside herself
all the parts
she'd thought
were missing

to my King

i believe in a you of loyalty
where you see your Queen and your children
as your own

where causing them pain and anguish
casts turmoil
on your own thrown

catch

here's a ball of my widest smiles

and the heaviest tears

collected painstakingly

all these years

wrapped in crippling, debilitating fears

and threads of hope

that the smoke clears

I threw it to you to see if you'd catch

your heart's already darkened

no match

my harshest critic

yet strongest supporter

shattered my soul

freed me through my slaughter

restless hollow legs

searching thinking winding weeping
falling stuttering climbing leaping
trap door
no floor
alarm sounds beeping
twisted insomnia
secrets keeping
inner hysteria
claustrophobia
spiders crawling
arachnophobia
unfulfilled stories
para ... noi ... i ... a
torment
torture
can't take no more of your ...

in the deepest ocean
in the clearest ocean blue
there i was for us
there you were for you

repellent

you'll walk with me to the edge of the water
where the waves break upon the sand
unable, or unwilling, to enter it
to be submerged with me, hand in hand

you will walk with me to the forest
but when the sun is dappled by the trees;
you turn back to rest in the sunshine,
while i ground, digging dirt, on my knees

i'll take the summit, i'll climb through the pain
i'll endure the sun, be replenished by the rain
when my muscles burn, i'll attract, i'll believe
a magnet repellent. when i push, you retrieve

make today's choices in awareness
of the consequences you and yours will be responsible for
in the future

see your choices in the power they offer you
to forge your paths ...

in addition
to the wounds that they will require you to suture

balance

if they want your advances and your money
but cannot see your worth
your relationship is in deficit
needing rebalancing and rebirth

make some investment guidelines
ensure dividends go both ways
or they'll leave when there's no more money
and you'll have spent more than just your pay

i wish you

love

light

and

happiness

just

not mine ...

that

left me

emptiness

compass

you mocked me in my happiness
never saw me in my gloom
i couldn't lift the clouds of your debilitating doom

i've built an inner tornado to rupture my bizarre state
to counteract each low blow
and counter the lingering hate

let it ravage my pre-conceptions
and let the landscape clear
I'm moving in new directions
you can keep your ingrained fear

*i dressed you
with words of affirmation
to raise you up, mr. tall*

*you undressed me
with lies and deceit
and traded me in, for a fall*

tempo

drum beat drum beat heart beat feet
heart beat heart beat drum beat heat
thumping thumping heaving chest
anticipation upon my breast
beating beating rising fast
fleeting moments never last
rising rising ever still
misinterpreted
silence
chill

a narcissist
will not see you
you are

just

another

stepping

stone

and
while you are
indebted to loyalty
they will always
be entitled to roam

result

what is pain
and what is grace
what is it to grieve
with a smile on your face

the humbled thief
given what he'd stole
he'd traded a diamond
for cast-away coal

she was just a girl
who loved a boy
that didn't see her

it was ...

devastating

realisation

straight laced
you covered your eyes for how many years
and bottled up your hopes
and dampened your dreams
and censored all of your deepest fears
so it never felt
" as bad as it seems "

... and when you finally opened your eyes
after smelling the burning of your skin
you verified all the scars from lies
you were burned by the fires of sin

... what then your investments of trust
unwavering as girlfriend and wife
cast aside for deceptions of lust...
paid for by half of your life

here and now

it's a hollow victory
arguing with your history
with contrary proof
here in the now, in the current day

keep living in the past
and your life will fly fast
how much more
will your soul have to pay

the VICTIM suffers from a situation not of their choosing. They decide to suffer the outcome.

The VICTOR sees the situation as a challenge to improve themselves:

- to stay positive in the face of immense loss, pain, struggle, depression or disappointment

- they believe that the experience is merely a moment in their story

- they are the heroine or hero of their story

- they do not choose to survive, they choose to rise to the challenge, to learn, to evolve, to strengthen, to fight, to live. not for revenge, but for love.
self-love and the love of others. the love of life and living with purpose. to fight, and live, another day

the VICTOR is victorious because in the face of a situation that demands that they shrink, the victor fuels themselves, rises to the challenge. then not only survives, but flourishes.
you see, the victor's story never ends.
what will you be?

be brave, be fierce, be kind. be you. be.

permission

you took me to the alter
held your lies under your breath
you'd already taken others
in our life before my death

i am not better than any others
nor can i stop from getting old
and life has not become
the plan my head once told

so here is a valid ticket
to leave me as you will
in spite of the promises we made
and the love i hold for you still

... and what is friendship
if you ripped my sails
broke my hull, cut away my anchor
and capsized my boat

you asked me to join your ship
and then pushed me off the plank ...
you saved and then drowned me ...

... what a blessing that i had taught myself to swim ...

cast

my eyes once shone
bright stars in a dark night sky
now earth bound puddles
are filled by the tears that i cry

how could i ever return to that place once on high
when i have lost the innocence of youth
and I have lost the ability to fly ...

the saddest part of finding one's true self
is that it simultaneously
demands the release of people in our lives
who threaten our ability
to live as our authentic selves

hollow

from the fullness of my womb
to the emptiness of my core
from the promise of everything
to the gut-wrenching no more

there are no words for the losses we feel
for the nightmares of missing parts
that we wish would prove real
the endings made of false starts

these are the unsung anguishes
of the women that deal
with unfulfilled fantasies
and real scars that won't heal

and what will you say

when your daughter is in tears

when some stupid boy

has confirmed all her fears

what will you say then

when history repeats

and all of your deceptions

are echoed by his deceits

karma

you can judge a book by its cover
but read it and discover
that we all wear an outer mask
to disguise our inner limitations
and our private lies ...

there are pros and cons
to everything
the fleeting affair
and the wedding ring
be careful the price
of integrity you sell
the universe knows
your kiss and tell

"what they don't know won't hurt them";
a coward curtails their consequences…
but, um…
you are responsible for your irresponsibility
and the ripples you cause in the sea
and if you see harm on the horizon
your polluting should never be done
do not muddy the waters of another's rivers
nature serves karma and it steadily delivers

deception

shallow are the women
who turn on their own kinds
feeding their own egos
trading their minds

as their souls fall behind them
with their karma in their wake
stealing fantasies that render
another's fortune fake

if he was only a woman's boy
then he was never an actual man
and because he fueled his own ego
he was never really their fan

home sweet home will not be a home
when you are single, and standing alone

you will watch her in respect
with belated gratitude and in awe

when she is up and she is leaving
and she is walking out the door

relationships

i thought you were my safe place

my hide-out

my rest stop

i thought i'd found a haven in your arms

a hill top

then deep drop ...

in a world of turmoil and endless demands

i thought i'd found love, held here in your hands

what I'd seen as a refuge

i would know as a cell

what i thought was protection

just a hollow shell

once an illusion

a romantic delusion

turned inner confusion

now foregone conclusion

i bid you farewell

*an illegitimate lover's legacy
loving a lover who's " already " in love
so they can be loved " by a lover "*

*inauthentic love is in losing ourselves,
and not having loved ourselves ...
that is a loss to discover*

*grieving the loss of the lover ...
languishing the loss of being loved ...
having traded ourselves for another*

mister

what will you call me
when your face is in the rain
praying to the gods
to wash away the pain

and what will you tell them
when they ask what you have done
who you traded for coal
in your search for the sun

*sometimes the things that break us
turn out to be the things that make us*

*the way we respond strengthens
and clarifies our existence*

*we can continue to grow
regardless roadblocks or resistance*

cremated

and now that you are ready
now that you are on my side
ready for me
to be your bride
for all the times we fought
you lied
for all the pain and times
i cried
for my heart and hands
you tore and tied
to the vows of respect
only i'd abide
the love i gave
that you burnt and dried
your smoke and mirrors
this love has died

she was so intent on giving
that she was blind to her experience of receiving
her intentions of giving happiness
resulted in malicious cause and
her own poetic injustice

freedom

if you're not a good husband
and i'm not a good wife
let's be each our own best
and separate our life

i love you enough to tell you
i'm not perfect on my own
but i'd prefer to be authentic,
be my inner best, full grown

in a minute i would liberate you
and give you freedom from our bind
from this 'now until our death'
that was only in my mind

i leeched upon your youth
when i dreamed us into existence
although i won you in the end
i should have listened to your resistance

i loved you tenderly
you savaged me with your bite
you took all our pleasant moments
and burned them in wicked light

when the jealous beating of your heart
tore our minds and our souls apart
when your sin of over needing
cut us both and left us bleeding

hope

swing low

sweet chariot

I'm not ready to part

don't hurry yet

i know death's counting seconds

round the corner

behind the door

tears on my hands

blood on this floor ...

and here in this breath

in my depths of despair

the soft weight of your body

the gleam of your hair

every intricate detail

now essential to clasp

before you lift and you leave me

falling out of my grasp

is the blame mine
or does it rest on you
that I never thought to test the things
you'd always said were true

is it on my shoulders
these 'steal' weighted boulders
of never being able to trust
i never found a protective love
just debilitating rust

hindsight

i take full responsibility
for leading you astray
for all the times i pleaded you
to make you want to stay

if i had acquired the wisdom
if i had been able to see
if i had really loved myself
i would have set you free

inks

remnant of your presence

blot my canvas

as stains and grazes

they rest

as marks

upon me

i navigate like mazes

song words

you've damaged my spirit
and ravaged my soul
all of your liberties
have taken their toll

where i once felt wholeness
now a vast gaping hole

and with what could i fill it
there's no remedy so strong
to forgive and forget
all that you have done wrong

i can drown in my tears
while i write you this song

i wish you well

but not from my well

and not of my wellness.

empty nesters

it's not that I don't love you
now the truth and pain has cleared
it's not that I don't love you
now life proved what I'd feared

it's not that I don't love you
now our children are all grown
it's just that now I realise
you were yours
i was my own

*mirror mirror on the wall
who is the happiest of them all?*

*"the ones
who do not need
my guiding reflection,
they embrace their beauty
and imperfection;*

*they know their worth is what is inside
and that is why they are most admired"*

from darker days

hiding demons
inside my head
muttering negatives
but nothing's said
deep dark thoughts
on which they're fed
the heavy poison
of bleeding lead
the struggle to live
when already dead

there is an anger in me that rages
uncleansed by the wisest of sages

mine is a heart that's been ravaged
a gentle soul, daggered and savaged

housed within my own good intentions
but devoid of rising ascensions
forgiveness is a word
I am incapable to say
in the darkest of realms
I am cursed to stay

exclusion

when we acknowledge our differences
we can see how we're the same
we can change our perspectives
stop this dead and mindless game

what did you intend
when you chose to cast me out
rendering me endangered
injured with self-doubt

did you enjoy your bright fame
shining, blinded by the light
your taste sweetened when opportunity came
and left a cruel and lingering bite

for some of us, life is a series of illusions dressed up in
achievements and material things;
of dreams come true packaged in cute babies clothes
and expensive diamond rings

… because when I thought all was safe and well
I dropped the furthest I could have fell
from all the lies you'd used as gel
of all the times you'd kissed, not tell

… but in my broken damaged heart
fires and smoke ignited my soul
I harnessed my remaining hope
for my most important role

… of all the dreams you'd shattered
and my innocence that you took
my children would never know that pain
they'd never read your book

… they would know of the power of belief
and a woman's courage to rise above
so where you sowed seeds of deceit
I would raise pillars of love

reclamation

incapacity

demands

mobility

departure

you can rise, here now beside me
or stay and fall behind
but I have no more stationary
no pause, stop or rewind

i've waited in your shadows
prayed you'd preach and join my name
but those visions have been shattered
and my mind rendered insane

i've climbed up out the wishing well
its depths hope couldn't break
now all the things i'd wished for
are mine to do and make

i wish you growth and love
and a change from deep within
i pray you see my light for you
I'm leaving as a gift, not sin

the universe, she taught to me
a better way to live and be
amazing grace, she gave to me
new eyes of clarity with which I see

master

love led me to the darkest deepest despair

rough

ragged

fallen

to fearfully aware

love led me to the pain of naive attachment

walking barefoot in the fire of re-enactment

love led me to the breathless, broken bottom

shivering

shaking

to fearfully forgotten

love led me to the paralysis of pain

clarity to isolation, to emotionally insane

love led me to the truth of my own existence

to the joy of inner strength and inner persistence

love led me to the integrity of taking responsibility

owning my own decisions. harnessing my ability

love led me through hell and into heaven's gate

love taught me that i am the master of my own fate

deal with the devil you know
or dance with the devil you don't
trust in time he will transcend
or retrace his records
he won't

will you savour the seeds you have so far sown
or sever your ties to claim the unknown

when love belies the believer
the giver redeems the rights of receiver

captain

you blinded me
i found the gift of sight
you cast me in darkness
i found my light
you disowned me
i found the will to fight
you censored me
i learnt to growl and bite
you cut me
i found renewal in my blood
you starved me
my thirst ignited a flood
you ravaged my flowers
i sprouted new bud
i created new life
from the crippling mud
and i thank you for all of the memories
that you ignored my begging, please
now i can sleep at peace with ease
i have navigated the roughest of seas

i am grateful for the growth
and the ability to change
for the music, once normal,
that has warped and is now strange

... because in that transient place
i was permitted to re-arrange
and found a life of authenticity
as a result of the exchange

phoenix

from the ashes of yesterday's fires
from the hollowed out well of unsated desires
from the pain of cheats, cowards and liars
from the treading of life's wearing tires
and all of the ill-fated pain that transpires

with the wisdom of hurdles
seen now cleared
of achievements made
although once feared
of scars now cooled
once raw and seared

of confidence in you
your truth revered
of your inner child
self-fed and reared

rise ... resurrected ... rise

choose courage and compassion
to combat conflict

challenge characteristics
to clarify cheats and cowards

do not fear being alone
if it leads you to your own

rebirth

so typically me
to bow down
to the most
insignificant tree
to flow through the years
'just as they'll be'
with some sort of unjustified reverie

to wake in a jolt of christened lightning
an absolution, bone-jarring, frightening
a snapping point into the freedom of wild
an essential encore of the inner child

where the struggles endured
were perceived pains to be cured
into new form
smelted by the sun
where the oddities of your past
no longer have grasp
and your ending is a life just begun

it's sadly sweet

to say goodbye

now I've the choice

to choose to try

i feel my soul

screech, cut and cry

when i ignore my truth

and live a lie

i'd best be bold

than stall and die

not to trim

but cut loose and fly

and if you should wonder

or ponder why

no, it's not an eye for an eye

it's just for me, myself and mine

i'm stepping out from behind your line

check mate

this is the last time you'll see me crumble

see me stumble

through my fears

with waivering values

and blurry vision

blinded with my tears

i've embraced my spark

my fire's burning ablaze

i can see through your smoke and mirrors

I see clearly your joker's maze

so thank you for the lessons

the scars gave me wisdom, harnessed intuition

i've mastered life's chess game

i am in charge of my position

*i called upon the angels
to cast some shining light
to bring with them some courage
to sustain me for the fight
they gazed upon me lovingly
they smiled and called me dear*

*"you have all you need already
your path has brought you here
take faith that we are with you
and that with the struggle
this fight will bring
clarity and purpose
there is timing for everything"*

fare-you-well

seek within a new beginning
the beauty of what is ending
welcome the cycle of seasons
and the growth, energy ascending

that in every shard of ice
and the frostbite of a frozen heart
is the warmth of hope and peace
that an inner love will start

the love back into your own keeping
the love of our guardian mother earth
the love of your permission for releasing
the self-love to accept your re-birth

... and there in the moment
of sink or swim
you can choose to end
or choose to begin

the path is never simply good versus sin;
where losers lose, and winners win

in the game of alchemy
you win with your heart
when in every ending
you accept a new start

conviction

"you are stronger than you look"
an inner acceptance is all it took
I reaffirmed my angle, leaned on my own hook
I am the heroine. I save myself in my own book

tell yourself the things that you need to hear
draw on your courage to challenge your fear
harness your voice
speak loud and speak clear
permit a smile upon your face
for each heartache and each tear

honestly

gratefully

i am not your 'supposed to be'

i couldn't do that

truthfully

and when I'm me

i'm youthfully

naturally

beautifully

everything

i wish to be

ravishing

soulfully

flying

free

tomorrow

there is hope
that the trap doors
of yester years

the torment
the anguish
the pain
the tears

will subside
washed-away
in a landslide

and the loyalty
of those
in whom you confide
will replace all of those
who deceived
and who lied

... and you can set free
the broken part of your heart
once kept in darkness
that died

it is not in the what
but in the how
that we are lost
and we are found

in the tearing of our souls
and in the gaping weeping holes
that we find the way to reattach ourselves
so we are stronger than before
breaking the limitations of our past
to unlock the future's door

and in our renovations
and in our restorations
we make new boundaries
and manifestations

child to adult to child to me

birthed as a whole. a soul cast into existing
moulded planned drafted written edited
(torn, shredded, burnt, scarred) erased
gathered, grieving, depressed, depleted, deleted

breathing. breathing. breathing. believing
peeling up from the floor. gathering strength
a step by step process. still gathering length
crawling. stumbling. walking. running. Fall ...

crawl. walk. run. step. breathe. stop
listen. breathe. stop. listen. breathe. believe. rise

child damaged. re-parented. me
breathe. be. breathe. be

it is in the sharing of your inner child

your genuine inner essence, the being in love and light

that children... and broken adults ...

find their own wings and can take flight

remuneration

in all my observations

of the world's steady rotations

of the suns and the skies and the sea

the day you were born right into my arms

that is still the most precious to me

indigo child

for Charlotte

you are the sun's salutation
to the night's passing tide
the perfect entrapment
life's essence, nature's pride

you are the belly shaking giggle
of the happiest child
the soulful enrapture
of the gypsy dancing wild

you are the sweetest taste of innocence
you have no idea the power you hold

you will not deny your inner child
fade in colour
nor grow old

persistence

for Gabrielle

you have the strike of a tigress
and the stubborn persistence of a bull
you are the curiosity of an eager mind
with the gentle touch of a spring lamb's wool

your beauty is met only
by the measure of your heart
large brown doe eyes
separate truth and lies apart

eyelash kisses tickling
and the loving caress of willing ears
i pray that your life meets you kindly
gifting heartfelt laughter and joyful tears

she

for Anastasia

you are the diamond dew

on a glistening winter morning

and the warmest rays of the shining summer sun

you are the sweet joy of a majestic melody

before the symphony has even begun

you are a sparkling effervescence

with an infectious inner chime

you are the fastest humming beat

yet your presence freezes time

child

i was scared for my babies
of being damaged and hurt
so i made them resilient
i made them alert

i let their expression
show who they truly are
rather than oppress them
change their expression to a scar

i can struggle to remember
that their choices are not mine
that there's a divine soul inside them
they know already how to shine

realignment

i didn't re-build myself up
brick by brick
so you could define me
with your incompetence to cope

you can take back your choices
(and your consequences)
you tied and bound yourself in this mess
you can learn to untie your own rope

remarkably

i watched my ego cut and run
lashing with its evil tongue
envious of others including the sun
leaving harm when said and done
i called it in and sat it down
curious what the inner talk found
discussed its need to fend and fight
the cause of the need to always be right
we spoke about the need to be
everything we think others see
to exist in the now to set us free
and that we are our own remarkably
to hold to our core values and our beliefs
to walk with the peasants and with the chiefs
that gratitude brings the clearest perspective
with love be overflowing, and rarely selective

maybe we could love again
start from the ground
instead of the sky
but this time
instead of falling in love
we will create a stable base
then build up on high

today

today. i stand. today. i ground
in the here. in the now
in the magic to be found

today. i am. unapologetically
in the body, mind and spirit
in the truth ready inside of me

today. i embrace, my unique shine
in the power and the strength
and the light that i call mine

today. i answer, my own call
like the echo of the chamber
i promise to catch me when i fall

they are not their past
as you are not yours
you are grown from your failures
to manifest new doors

so evaluate in this moment
do they love you from their heart
only that truth divides supporters
and critics apart

scoring

say it " I am not who I was
and they are not who they were before "
if you can settle in the here and now
you can abstain from keeping score

there is a purity and a private peace
from letting what was be as it may
instead of adding up the numbers
of who did what and who should pay

... because if you hold them to your yesterday
you tax yourself of your tomorrow
when you invest in your pain and loss
your inner being will end up hollow

will you, will you heed my call
hold my hand to stop my fall
will you listen with open ears
clear your mind and share my fears
could you, could you hold me down
keep me safe and keep me sound
open my eyes, so that i can see
i am already all that i need to be

dusk dawn; faith reform

i'll meet you in the middle
on the dark side of the moon
to share our perspectives,
align our frequencies, attune

i'll dance in the darkness
to bring forth the light
brace the sun's warmth
to farewell the night

we will meet at the horizon
on the bend of dusk and dawn
we can bathe in the moon dust
and shed, new skins, re-born

we'll relish in the moonlight
whilst savouring the sun
to confirm our resolution
and resolve to being one

... and with love, but not in it
you will find an amplifying energy
of enhancement and serenity
let it breathe within and through you
but let it not consume you
let it verify your consciousness
and transcend energies from old to new ...
but maintain your fullness
and being centred on your own
maintain your own space
in which to breathe and roam

time out

if I leave here tomorrow
I hope you chase away the pain
with the time we spent together
and that I will see you once again

the reason I must leave you
is to keep you safe from harm
to chase away my demons
and return to cupid's calm

when I love you so fiercely
it pains me to stay in sight
when my need of you is two-fold
separation from wrong is right

*i'm going to say that i see you and stop saying that
i 'love' you;
because those word are now irrelevant.
i'm going to say i believe in you and the parts you leave
unseen; your insecurity, behind your arrogant
... because love is a deranged word
with commercial connotations
and what i feel for you is a universal binding ...
set in the pit of my stomach
in the beating of my heart
in the coding of my dna
like the ocean waves that lap the shore
and the wind that caresses the trees
in the scorching heat that penetrates
the biting cold of the snowy mountain's freeze,
in the newborns harnessing arrival
and in the wisdom of the turning of tides
in the seeds that spring to abundance
and the knowing clock that chimes
i something more than love you
i've known you for a thousand years
through ages toiled and lands explored
we are carved in sweat and tears*

separately

me to mine and you to yours

to unwrap our hiding, hidden flaws

to walk through

instead of closing doors

and as the paths

we choose come clear

you'll find your there

I'll find my here

we'll choose authentic

and face our fear ...

and if in the end we find ourselves

in different places on different shelves

you be you

they'll be themselves

and i hope you find

all that you can be

and your life has truth, love and clarity

whether it's together

or separately

*let me find my peace with you
though you stopped my beating heart
and though i wanted no more from you
time mends broken ends, to restart...*

*i'm sorting still the days months years
of my own unhappiness and of my tears
revisiting my childhood and within my youth
seeing as an adult, life's deceptions and truth*

*... but of all the hurt you chose to bestow
my love and gratitude continues to grow;
for all the times you discarded me
I've rebirthed myself my reality.*

moving on

i wrote him a book of poetry to credit his deceit

and explore my being butchered

as yet another piece of meat ...

so here is a poem to credit that stage

i've decided it's now complete ...

and now i am sure of who i am

i have no reason to compete

when i answer my own calling

i am my only true defeat

THE END

&

THE BEGINNING

butterfly

i painted a picture, i painted with words
once caged souls, now sky soaring birds
i kept in a jar in the shape of a heart
a ball for each hope and each love torn apart

a heaviness deep of the seas ocean blue
opportunities for peace, each long overdue
contained in clear glass, secured with a lid
a facade to contain all the hurts that were hid

then today i decided that i'd let them go
for years they'd amounted, i'd never said no
i'd kept them as souvenirs of people i'd known
some that had left me, others i had outgrown

to create new space i let go of the weight
replacing love and empathy to each stabbing hate
i farewelled the dark depths keeping me low
for too long they'd hindered my movement and glow
as i opened the lid and i bid them goodbye
in place of each ball, flew a blue butterfly

A Final Word: To the Warrior Women

to all of the women
re-owning internal rights
in replace of exhausting,
masculine induced fights
as the flames are burning brighter
with our burdens getting lighter
start embracing your flight ready wings
and your gifted, wondrous soul, she still sings
amassed with pure love
and the right to explore
charged by the fire
at the centre of your core
with your roots firmly planted in the soil
and your crown upon your head, you were always royal

– – – – – – – –

breathe with your heart, inhale your sacred gift
your unique talents allow you to shape shift
embrace what you knew, and yet you disowned
your divinity is embedded, it was never loaned
embark on your journey to release your inner you
all hail the wild women, long awaited, long overdue

don't ask " when were you born? "
ask " when did you show up? "

" what happened to break you so deeply
that it ripped you from your core ...
that you were born again?
born out of societies hold
and back into your own safe keeping
back into your spiritual soul "

don't wait for the wake up

show up

be seen

be true

be you

grant yourself permission to self-learn and align,

harnessing your inner glory, gifted by the divine,

to rise now, as you are, a diamond in the rough;

you have always been more than enough

PERMISSION SLIP

I _____ (insert full name) re-birth my-self back into my own safe keeping. I grant permission to rediscover the true sense of my soul. I call back the parts of my being that I have discarded. I commit to living an enriched, authentic life that honors the soul within me; the being I was before I allowed myself to be edited, shape shifted, bullied into an altered format.

I commit to taking personal responsibility for my body and my mind, by taking time for myself. Time to sit in stillness, creating space to connect with my inner spirit, my soul and my connection with the higher powers and their energies. Time to move so that I can enjoy the gift of my physical body. Just as I am. To my levels. There is nothing missing.

I value my relationship with myself. I am kind to myself. I evaluate the things that I enjoy, or do not enjoy. The foods that I like and do not like; those foods that empower me or drain me. I listen to how my body feels when I treat it in particular ways. I love every part of me. I am proud of who I am and what I am. I have much to offer the world. I am a unique gift to the world. The world will benefit from what I have to offer when I am my authentic self. I promise to harness my best version of myself. The unique expression of my inner being. Just as I am.

_____

SIGNED: DATE:

release

www.ingramcontent.com/pod-product-compliance
Lightning Source LLC
Chambersburg PA
CBHW051953290426
44110CB00015B/2223